Colli...

W...

Handwriting

Jenny Siklós

Collins

HarperCollins Publishers
77–85 Fulham Palace Road
Hammersmith
London W6 8JB

First edition 2012

Reprint 10 9 8 7 6 5 4 3 2 1 0

Produced for HarperCollins by:
White-Thomson Publishing Ltd.
0843 208 7460
www.wtpub.co.uk

Editor: Alice Harman
Layout designer: Kim Williams

ISBN 978-0-00-746942-0

www.collinselt.com

A catalogue record for this book is available from the British Library.

Printed in China by South China Printing Co.

The publishers would like to thank John Walsh of BEBC for suggesting
the idea for this book, and Tammy Poggo for her advice during the
early development stages.

Picture credits:
page 8 (top): Feng Yu; page 8 (bottom): Stephen Aaron Rees; page
8 (bottom inset) Phant; page 9 (top): Julija Sapic; page 9 (bottom):
thepencilgrip.com; page 10, page 32: Ingvar Bjork; page 33: astudio;
page 36: Brian Weed; page 73: Lars Lindblad; page 74, page 75: juat.

Contents

1

How to use this book

Welcome to *Work on your Handwriting*!

This is a practical workbook to help you work on your handwriting in English. You will learn how to correctly write all upper-case and lower-case letters, and how to form words so that they are clear and neat. You will practise using proper spacing and punctuation in sentences and paragraphs, so that your handwriting is easy for others to read.

You may find that writing in English is very different to writing in your own language, especially if you usually write from right to left and/or use another alphabet. You can improve your handwriting by looking carefully at the examples in this book, and completing the practice exercises.

The book is designed to work in different ways. For example, you can start at the beginning of the book and work your way through to the end. Or, if you have specific areas of handwriting that you want to work on, you can pick and choose the parts of the book that practise these skills.

Most important of all: you will get back what you put in. If you practise regularly, you will change your handwriting faster. If you don't, you won't. It's simple, really.

You can use *Work on your Handwriting*:

- as a self-study course
- with a teacher in a classroom

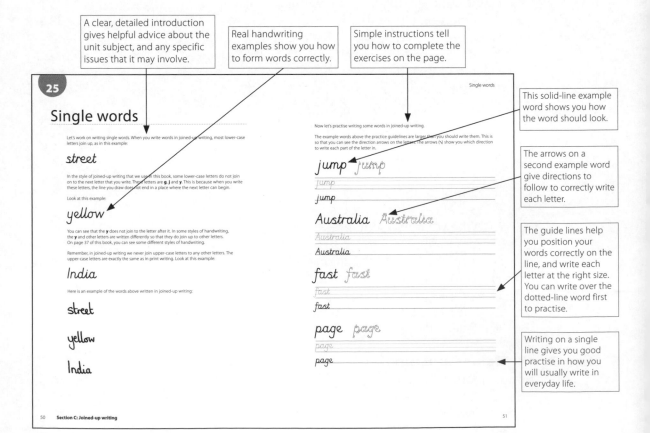

A clear, detailed introduction gives helpful advice about the unit subject, and any specific issues that it may involve.

Real handwriting examples show you how to form words correctly.

Simple instructions tell you how to complete the exercises on the page.

This solid-line example word shows you how the word should look.

The arrows on a second example word give directions to follow to correctly write each letter.

The guide lines help you position your words correctly on the line, and write each letter at the right size. You can write over the dotted-line word first to practise.

Writing on a single line gives you good practise in how you will usually write in everyday life.

How this book works

This book has four sections:

- Section A introduces the tools and skills you need for good handwriting in English.
- Section B looks at print writing. Print writing is very important to use in many official situations – for example, when you fill in forms.
- Section C looks at joined-up writing. You will use joined-up writing for most situations, from taking notes in class to writing a thank-you note.
- Section D has games that you can play, to practise your handwriting and have some fun at the same time.

Print writing and joined-up writing

It is important that you learn how to correctly use the two types of handwriting in English – print writing and joined-up writing.

In the print section, you will:

- learn how to write each letter of the alphabet correctly
- practise writing each letter
- work on writing letters with ascenders and descenders
- practise writing numbers
- learn about upper-case letters
- work on correct spacing between words
- learn about punctuation
- do free-writing exercises

In the joined-up writing section, you will:

- learn how to write each letter of the alphabet correctly
- practise writing each letter
- work on writing letter pairs
- practise writing words and groups of words
- learn to write sentences with correct spacing and punctuation
- practise writing sentences that include numbers
- work on writing paragraphs
- do free-writing exercises

Common problems with handwriting

Many students have problems with their handwriting when they begin to write in English. This is normal. Everything you do in English needs practice!

The most common mistakes that students make in handwriting are shown below. When you practise handwriting, try not to make these mistakes.

Here are some examples of the mistakes teachers often see in class:

- The letters are not the same size.

He iS RUSSian.

- There are unequal spaces between words.

Is it raining?

- Letters and words are not written in a straight line.

The boy is happy.

This page shows you examples of good handwriting that does not include common mistakes. With practice, you can write like this too.

- The sizes of the upper-case letters are the same. The sizes of the lower-case letters are also the same.

He is Russian.

- There are equal spaces between the words.

Is it raining?

- The words go along a straight line.

The boy is happy.

Tips for good handwriting

Writing tools

It is important to have good tools to practise your handwriting. You should have good-quality pencils and rubbers for practice, and a pencil sharpener. Make sure you use HB pencils, known as No. 2 pencils in other areas of the world.

Pencils are best for handwriting practice as you can erase any mistakes you make. You should also have a pen, so that you can practise writing with this too. It is a good idea to keep all your writing tools together in a pencil case.

Notebooks and paper

Students sometimes use very small notebooks. These are not good for handwriting practice because there isn't enough space on each page to work.

Make sure that your notebook has standard A4-sized pages of lined paper.

Holding the pen or pencil correctly

To write well, you must make sure you hold the pen or pencil correctly.

Here is an example of the 'tripod' grip, the most common way of holding a pen or pencil when writing in English. The hand position is the same whether you use your right hand or your left hand to write.

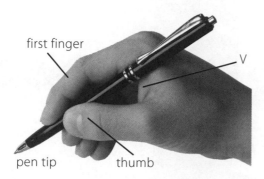

right-handed tripod grip　　　　**left-handed tripod grip**

Rest the pen in the 'V' between your thumb and first finger. Hold the pen between your thumb, first finger and middle finger. Put your first finger on top of the pen, and your middle finger and thumb on each side of the pen. Your fingers should be 1 or 2 cm away from the pen tip.

Pencil grips

Students sometimes have problems holding onto a thin pencil or pen. You can buy things called pencil grips to help with this. Pencil grips can also make it more comfortable to write for a long period of time.

There are many different types of pencil grips. You can buy them in a stationer's shop (a shop that sells writing tools and materials), or you can buy them on the internet.

Here is an example of one kind of pencil grip:

Introduction to print writing

Print writing is used when handwriting needs to be extremely clear and easy to read – for example, when writing details on a luggage tag that goes on a suitcase when you travel.

Print writing should always be used for official forms, such as job applications, that we use to give important information about ourselves. Many of these forms are looked at (scanned) by computers and must be very easy to read.

Application for Employment

Position applied for: _Office Administrator_

Name: _Amy Yu_

Address: _5 Wightman Road, Edinburgh EH4 8QS_

Email: _amy.yu.1985.edin@mail.com_   Mobile: _07825 116 413_

Give details of your most recent employment:

Position: _Receptionist_   Name of business or employer: _Ciscenta Sales_

Dates of employment: _01/03/2009 – present_   Rate of pay: _£18,000 p.a._

What were your duties? _Greeting visitors, answering telephones and directing calls to different departments, opening and distributing post, filing, keeping client contact information up to date._

Print letters

There are 26 letters in the English alphabet. On this page, you can see how the upper-case and lower-case letters look in print writing.

Upper-case letters (also called capital letters):

A B C D E F G

H I J K L M N O

P Q R S T U V

W X Y Z

Lower-case letters (also called small letters):

a b c d e f g

h i j k l m n o

p q r s t u v

w x y z

Print letters Aa–Ee

We will start by practising the print letters. It is important to form single letters correctly before moving on to writing words and sentences. We will practise both upper-case (**A**) and lower-case (**a**) letters.

The example letters above the practice guidelines are larger than you should write them. This is so that you can see the direction arrows on the letters. The arrows (↘) show you which direction to write each part of the letter in. Sometimes the arrows have numbers, to tell you which part of the letter to write first and when to lift your pen to start a new part of the letter. If there is only a number 1, write the letter without lifting your pen from the paper.

A a A a

Now practise your **A** and **a** on a single line.

A

a

B b B b

Now practise your **B** and **b** on a single line.

B

b

C c C c

C

c

Now practise your **C** and **c** on a single line.

C

c

D d D d

D

d

Now practise your **D** and **d** on a single line.

D

d

E e E e

E

e

Now practise your **E** and **e** on a single line.

E

e

Print letters Ff–Kk

Practise writing each letter on the guidelines and the single lines underneath.

F f

F

f

F

f

G g

G

g

G

g

H h

H

h

H

h

I i

J j

K k

Print letters Ll–Qq

Practise writing each letter on the guidelines and the single lines underneath.

L l L l

L
l

M m M m

M

m

M
m

N n N n

N

n

N
n

O o   O o

O

o

P p   P p

P

P

P

p

Q q   Q q

Q

q

Q

q

Print letters Rr–Ww

Practise writing each letter on the guidelines and the single lines underneath.

R r R r

R

r

S s S s

S

s

S

s

T t T t

T

t

T

t

U u U u

U

u

U

u

V v V v

V

v

V

v

W w W w

W

w

W

w

Print letters Xx–Zz

Practise writing each letter on the guidelines and the single lines underneath.

X x X x

Y y Y y

Z z Z z

Different writing styles

On this page, let's look at some different ways that people can write letters. In this book, you are learning one style of handwriting, in print and joined-up forms. But there are many other styles that people use, and they are also correct. It is important to know that letters do not always look the same, and to be able to recognise letters that are formed differently from the ones you write.

Upper-case **I**:

Italy   Italy

Upper-case **M**:

Mr Porter   Mr Porter

Upper-case **W**:

Wales   Wales

Lower-case **y**:

yellow   yellow

Lower-case **z**:

zoo   zoo

Ascenders and descenders

Many letters are all the same height. They fit between the baseline and the meanline. You can see this in the example below:

baseline — *same* — meanline

But some letters have parts that go above the meanline. These parts are called ascenders. The letter **d** has an ascender:

— ascender

door

Other letters have descenders. These are parts of the letter that go below the baseline. The letter **y** has a descender:

descender

many

Now let's practise writing words that include letters with ascenders or descenders.

The example words above the practice guidelines are larger than you should write them. This is so that you can see the direction arrows on the letters. The arrows (↘) show you which direction to write each part of the letter in. Sometimes the arrows have numbers, to tell you which part of the letter to write first and when to lift your pen to start a new part of the letter. If there is only a number 1, write the letter without lifting your pen from the paper.

food   *food*

food

food

Now practise writing **food** on a single line. Keep the ascenders and descenders the same length.

food

Practise writing some words with ascender and descender letters. Try to keep the ascenders and descenders the same length every time.

angry   angry

angry

angry

joke   joke

joke

joke

table   table

table

table

happy   happy

happy

happy

quiet   quiet

quiet

quiet

Numbers

In print writing and joined-up writing, we write numbers in the same way.

The example numbers above the single practice lines are larger than you should write them. This is so that you can see the direction arrows on the numbers. The arrows (↘) show you which direction to write each part of the number in. Sometimes the arrows have numbers beside them, to tell you which part of the number to write first and when to lift your pen to start a new part of the number. If there is only a number 1, write the number without lifting your pen from the paper.

1

1

2

2

3

3

4

4

5

5

6   6

6 _____

7   7

7 _____

Sometimes people write the number 7 with a line through it, to make clear that it is not a number 1. This is what this type of number 7 looks like: 7

8   8

8 _____

9   9

9 _____

0   0

0 _____

Words with upper-case letters

You will use print writing to fill in official forms, such as job applications. In these forms, you will often have to use words that start with upper-case letters.

In English, you have to use upper-case letters to begin names of people, countries, cities and towns, days of the week, months, roads, companies and organisations, and some special buildings (such as Buckingham Palace or the Eiffel Tower). When writing about jobs, job titles should begin with a capital letter – for example, Managing Director.

When you practise writing words that begin with upper-case letters, remember that the upper-case letters sit on the baseline and do not go below it.

The example words above the practice guidelines are larger than you should write them. This is so that you can see the direction arrows on the letters. The arrows (↘) show you which direction to write each part of the letter in. Sometimes the arrows have numbers, to tell you which part of the letter to write first and when to lift your pen to start a new part of the letter. If there is only a number 1, write the letter without lifting your pen from the paper.

John Smith   John Smith

John Smith

John Smith

Saudi Arabia   Saudi Arabia

Saudi Arabia

Saudi Arabia

New York   New York

New York

New York

Tuesday Tuesday

Tuesday

Tuesday

20 December 20 December

20 December

20 December

Oxford Street Oxford Street

Oxford Street

Oxford Street

Red Cross Red Cross

Red Cross

Red Cross

Taj Mahal Taj Mahal

Taj Mahal

Taj Mahal

Spacing

Now let's do some more work on writing two or more words. Remember to make a space between each word. Spacing is very important when writing in English.

To use spacing correctly:

• make one space between each word (like the size of an **a**)

• make your spaces the same size every time

If you get the spacing wrong, it will be difficult for people to read your writing and understand what you are trying to say.

Here is an example of good spacing:

a■sunny■day

Look at the spacing. The grey area shows how big the space between each word should be. These words are all spaced well. The reader can understand what the student is writing.

Here are two examples of incorrect spacing:

asunny■day

What is the problem here? All words, including short ones like **a**, **an** and **the**, need a space between them and the next word.

a■sunny■■day

In this example, the space after 'sunny' is too big. Remember, the spaces should be the same size between every word.

Now you can practise for yourself. As you practise first with the dotted words, make sure that your letters do not touch the grey space. Then, when you write letters without the dotted outlines, imagine a grey space of that size between every word.

The example letters above the practice guidelines are larger than you should write them. This is so that you can see the direction arrows on the letters. The arrows (↘) show you which direction to write each part of the letter in. Sometimes the arrows have numbers, to tell you which part of the letter to write first and when to lift your pen to start a new part of the letter. If there is only a number 1, write the letter without lifting your pen from the paper.

a sunny day

a sunny day

two students

two students

in the office

in the office

a large family

a large family

Punctuation

When you write sentences in English, you have to use punctuation. Punctuation gives more information to the reader. The punctuation marks that you can practise on this page are:

- full stop
, comma
, apostrophe

! exclamation mark
? question mark

You need to make sure that you write punctuation marks correctly, so that the reader can understand the extra information that the punctuation gives.

Here are two examples of incorrect punctuation:

He lives in Manchester.

This full stop is much too big. It should be the same size as the dot on the lower-case **i**.

She has two horses.

This full stop looks like a small **o**, but it should be a dot, with no hole inside.

Here is an example of correct punctuation:

I am scared of spiders.

This full stop is the right size, and it has been formed correctly as a solid dot.

Practise writing each of these punctuation marks on guidelines. The example punctuation marks above the practice guidelines are larger than you should write them. This is so that you can see the direction arrows on the punctuation marks. The arrows (↘) show you which direction to write each part of the punctuation mark in. Sometimes the arrows have numbers beside them, to tell you which part of the punctuation mark to write first and when to lift your pen to start a new part of the punctuation mark. If there is only a number 1, write the punctuation mark without lifting your pen from the paper.

'Real world' print writing exercises 1

Now let's practise your print handwriting in 'real world' situations. This will help you when you need to clearly write important information in your everyday life.

Luggage labels

It is important to write clearly on a luggage label. If people cannot read the information you have written, they may not know that your suitcase belongs to you!

Fill out this luggage label with the information below:

Name: Karim Jones
Address: 3 High Street, Bedford MK42 A3E
Country: United Kingdom
Telephone: 07825 116 413

Name

Address

Country

Telephone

Letters

You will often have to write clearly and carefully without guidelines or blank boxes to help you – for example, when you want to send a letter to someone, and you have to write his or her address on an envelope.

Let's practise this situation on the envelope below. The arrows show the place in the centre of the envelope where you can write the name and address. Be careful to keep the words in a straight line.

Write this name and address on the envelope below:

Mr Owen Harris
112 Gatsby Way
London
W12 8BD
United Kingdom

'Real world' print writing exercises 2

Simple application forms

Here is an example of a simple application form for a gym membership. Complete this form with your personal details, such as your name and your address.

Make sure you write inside the right space on the form, and keep your writing straight so that it is neat and easy to read.

The instruction at the top of this form asks you to write your answers in block capitals (upper-case letters). We don't usually write words all in upper-case letters, but quite a lot of forms ask you to do this. It makes your writing clearer for the people who are reading the form.

FitLife Gym

Application Form

Please complete this form in block capitals.

Name _____

Address _____

_____

_____

Phone _____

Date of birth _____

Email _____

Why do you want to join this gym? _____

_____

_____

_____

_____

_____

Job application forms

Now let's practise writing a job application form. Look carefully at what information you need to write in each space on the form. Make sure you plan enough space for everything you have to write! Look at the example job application on page 10 to help you fill in the form correctly.

On this form, there is no instruction to write all in capital (upper-case) letters. This means that you can write words in lower-case letters, and only use upper-case letters at the start of a sentence and to begin certain types of words. Turn to page 26 to see a list of these types of words.

Application for Employment

Position applied for: _____

Name: _____

Address: _____

_____

Email: _____ Mobile: _____

Give details of your most recent employment:

Position: _____

Name of business or employer: _____

Dates of employment: _____ Rate of pay: _____

What were your duties? _____

_____

_____

Please give details of your education and qualifications:

Name and address of school or university/college	Qualifications (e.g. BA Hons in Business Studies)
_____ _____ _____	_____ _____ _____

Why do you want to work for us? _____

_____

_____

_____

Introduction to joined-up writing

Joined-up writing is a type of handwriting that you can use for most everyday writing. You should use joined-up writing when you write notes and letters to people.

It is also best to use joined-up writing when you need to write quickly and well – for example, when you take notes in a classroom or make a shopping list. Correct joined-up writing allows you to write quickly in a way that is still easy to read, and makes your writing look more advanced.

Here is an example of a thank-you note in neat joined-up writing:

Dear Alex,

Thank you so much for inviting me to dinner with your family. You have beautiful children, and such a lovely home. The meal was delicious. One day soon, I will invite you to my home for traditional Chinese food.

Yours,

Shih-Fang

Here is an example of neat classroom notes from a university student:

English Class – first lesson

Teacher – Kieran Bale
Homework every day
Read 3 chapters of textbook per week
Journal – must hand in on Fridays
Problems? Ask after class or email
Group presentations once a week

Joined-up letters

There are 26 letters in the English alphabet. On this page, you can see how the lower-case letters can look in joined-up writing.

In joined-up writing, it is only the lower-case letters that join to each other. The upper-case letters do not join at all. They are exactly the same as print upper-case letters.

Lower-case letters (also called small letters):

a b c d e f g
h i j k l m n
o p q r s t u
v w x y z

Here are some examples of different kinds of joined-up writing. Every person writes in his or her own way. It is important that you can read and understand other people's handwriting, even if it is a bit different to what you have seen before. As your handwriting improves, you can change your own way of writing too, to make your own style.

I go to the gym twice a week.

Do you need any help?

I can't remember his name.

It's my birthday on Tuesday!

Joined-up letters a–g

Let's practise writing joined-up letters. It is important to write single letters correctly before moving on to writing words and sentences.

Upper-case letters (**A**) do not join up. For this reason, you will practise only lower-case letters (**a**) in the joined-up letters section.

The example letters above the practice guidelines are larger than you should write them. This is so that you can see the direction arrows on the letters. The arrows (↘) show you which direction to write each part of the letter in. Sometimes the arrows have numbers, to tell you which part of the letter to write first and when to lift your pen to start a new part of the letter. If there is only a number 1, write the letter without lifting your pen from the paper.

a *a*

a

Now practise your **a** on a single line.

a

b *b*

b

Now practise your **b** on a single line.

b

c *c*

c

Now practise your **c** on a single line.

c

d

d

Now practise your **d** on a single line.

d

e   *e*

e

Now practise your **e** on a single line.

e

f   *f*

f

Now practise your **f** on a single line.

f

g   *g*

g

Now practise your **g** on a single line.

g

Joined-up letters h–o

h   h

Now practise your **h** on a single line.

h

i   i

Now practise your **i** on a single line.

i

j   j

Now practise your **j** on a single line.

j

k   k

Now practise your **k** on a single line.

k

l *l*

Now practise your **l** on a single line.

l

m *m*

Now practise your **m** on a single line.

m

n *n*

Now practise your **n** on a single line.

n

o *o*

Now practise your **o** on a single line.

o

Joined-up letters p–w

p p

Now practise your **p** on a single line.

p

q q

Now practise your **q** on a single line.

q

r r

Now practise your **r** on a single line.

r

s s

Now practise your **s** on a single line.

s

t *t*

t

Now practise your **t** on a single line.

t

u *u*

u

Now practise your **u** on a single line.

u

v *v*

v

Now practise your **v** on a single line.

v

w *w*

w

Now practise your **w** on a single line.

w

Joined-up letters x–z

x x

x

Now practise your **x** on a single line.

x

y y

y

Now practise your **y** on a single line.

y

z z

z

Now practise your **z** on a single line.

z

Practise each of the lower-case joined-up letters again here. Write in the space next to each example letter:

a b c d e f g h i j k l m
n o p q r s t u v w x y z

Letter pairs ch th wh

In joined-up writing, you connect – or join – most of the letters when you write a word. Now that you have practised writing single joined-up letters, you can move on to writing letter pairs – two letters that go together. On this page, let's practise writing **ch**, **th** and **wh**.

The example letters above the practice guidelines are larger than you should write them. This is so that you can see the direction arrows on the letters. The arrows (↘) show you which direction to write each part of the letter in.

ch   ch

Now practise your **ch** on a single line.

ch

th   th

Now practise your **th** on a single line.

th

wh   wh

Now practise your **wh** on a single line.

wh

Letter pairs bl cl pl cr dr fr

bl *bl*

bl

Now practise your **bl** on a single line.

bl

cl *cl*

cl

Now practise your **cl** on a single line.

cl

pl *pl*

pl

Now practise your **pl** on a single line.

pl

Practise writing the **bl** letter pair in the word **blue**:

blue *blue*

blue

Now practise the word **blue** on a single line.

blue

cr   cr

cr

Now practise your **cr** on a single line.

cr

dr   dr

dr

Now practise your **dr** on a single line.

dr

fr   fr

fr

Now practise your **fr** on a single line.

fr

Practise writing the **dr** letter pair in the word **drive**:

drive   drive

drive

Now practise the word **drive** on a single line.

drive

Letter pairs

sm sn sp er es ng

Letter pairs have special joins and are very important to practise. Here you will practise each pair on its own on guidelines. Underneath this, you will write out an example word that includes the letter pair.

sm   *sm*

sm

small

small

sn   *sn*

sn

snake

snake

sp   *sp*

sp

spelling

spelling

er   er

er

sister

sister

es   es

es

washes

washes

ng   ng

ng

king

king

Single words

Let's work on writing single words. When you write words in joined-up writing, most lower-case letters join up, as in this example:

street

In the style of joined-up writing that we use in this book, some lower-case letters do not join on to the next letter that you write. These letters are **g**, **j** and **y**. This is because when you write these letters, the line you draw does not end in a place where the next letter can begin.

Look at this example:

yellow

You can see that the **y** does not join to the letter after it. In some styles of handwriting, the **y** and other letters are written differently so that they do join up to other letters. On page 37 of this book, you can see some different styles of handwriting.

Remember, in joined-up writing we never join upper-case letters to any other letters. The upper-case letters are exactly the same as in print writing. Look at this example:

India

Here is an example of the words above written in joined-up writing:

street

yellow

India

Now let's practise writing some words in joined-up writing.

The example words above the practice guidelines are larger than you should write them. This is so that you can see the direction arrows on the letters. The arrows (↘) show you which direction to write each part of the letter in.

jump jump

jump

jump

Australia Australia

Australia

Australia

fast fast

fast

fast

page page

page

page

Punctuation and spacing

The rules for correct spacing with punctuation marks are the same when you use print writing or joined-up writing:

- There is never a space before the punctuation mark.
- There is always a single space after the punctuation mark.

This means that there is always a single space between each sentence that we write. A punctuation mark never joins up with the letter before it.

Here is an example of correct spacing between sentences:

The dog is hungry.█We need to feed it.█I will buy some food.

In each sentence, there is no space between the full stop and the letter before it. The full stop is also not joined to the letter before it. There is a single space after each full stop, and this means that there is one space between each sentence.

Here is an example of incorrect spacing in a sentence:

The dog is hungry.██We need to feed it.I will buy some food█.

At the end of the first sentence, there are two spaces between the full stop and the letter after it. There is no space between the last two sentences. In the third sentence, there is a space between the full stop and the letter before it.

Now let's practise writing sentences with correct spacing, on the guidelines below the example and then on the single lines:

I'm going on holiday. Amira, John and Taiki are coming too.

I work in East London. Where do you work? Do you like it?

Are you coming to the park? It is so sunny today!

Sentences

When you feel that you have practised enough with letters and words, you can move on to writing sentences.

As you write your sentences, remember the basic things that you must do:

- Make sure that your letters are the same size and shape each time you write them.
- Be careful to make your ascenders and descenders touch the top and bottom guidelines. Remember where these guidelines would be when you write on a single line.
- Keep equal spaces between words (see pages 28–29 for more help with this).
- Use a full stop, question mark or exclamation mark at the end of every sentence.

Write on the guidelines and the single line below each example sentence.

The train is late.

Do you travel a lot for work?

My favourite TV show is on tonight.

What is your name?

I have lived in Japan, France and Russia.

It is raining again today!

She plays football, tennis and squash.

He likes going to the theatre.

Complete the sentences

Now let's practise writing parts of sentences without using guidelines. You will write on a single line straight away, like when you write in a standard notebook. This practice will help you to write your letters at an equal size, and to use the correct spacing between words.

On this page, write the missing words into the sentences, so that they match the example above.

I like to eat but not to cook!

I like to ___ but not to cook!

What do you like doing at the weekend?

What do you _____ the weekend?

She goes shopping every Saturday.

She _____ every _____.

Do you live near here?

_____ live near ____?

I go running three times a week.

I _____ three times _____.

On this page, fill in the blank spaces with the typed words above the sentence. The words are not in order, so sometimes you have to decide where you think each word fits in the sentence.

In some of the sentences, each word can go in more than one space. In others, the sentence only makes sense when the words are in specific spaces.

pasta   tomatoes   cheese

I need to buy _____, _____ and _____ .

Italy   China

She is from _____. She wants to visit _____ .

work   relaxing

On Sundays, I like _____. I don't like having to ____ .

win the lottery   easy

I would love to _____. I would have a very ____ life!

Sentences with numbers

On these pages, let's practise writing full sentences that include numbers as well as letters. Remember that numbers do not join up to each other. Numbers also never join up to letters.

Write each sentence on the single line under the example.

She is 24 years old.

_____

I will call you back in 5 minutes.

_____

Shilpa was born on 5 July 1997.

_____

More than 8,000,000 people live in London.

_____

There were 30,000 people at the festival.

_____

Money symbols in sentences

When you write about amounts of money, you need to use money symbols. Here are three of the most common money symbols:

£ UK sterling (pound)

€ Eurozone euro

$ US dollar

First, practise writing the money symbols. Be careful to place them correctly on the baseline, and to write them at an equal size each time. It is important that these money symbols are clear and easy to read.

Now practise using these money symbols with numbers in sentences. Write each sentence on the single line under the example.

The flight costs £800.

I can't believe this handbag is $500!

Write your own sentences

Now you will practise writing sentences about yourself. On these pages, there are sentences that give information about a person and then ask you for the same information.

Write your answer as a full sentence on the single line below the question. Here is an example to help you:

Khalida lives in a large house in London. Where do you live?

I live in a flat in Brighton.

As you write, remember to:

- Be careful about your handwriting. Don't worry about grammar or vocabulary.
- Start each sentence with an upper-case letter.
- Make your letters the same size.
- Make ascenders and descenders the same length.
- Keep equal spaces between words.
- Finish your sentences with a full stop.

Chinese and Italian foods are both very popular around the world. What is your favourite type of food?

_____

Many people like to go to the cinema at the weekend. What do you usually do at the weekend?

_____

Mohammed's dad's name is Saleh. What's your dad's name?

_____

Lee loves watching football. What sport do you love watching?

_____

Many people dream of travelling around the world. If you could travel anywhere, where would you go?

_____

Brothers and sisters are called siblings. How many siblings, or brothers and sisters, do you have?

_____

There are good things about every season. What do you like best about summer?

_____

Some people have a party on their birthday. What do you usually do on your birthday?

_____

31

Paragraphs

When you feel that you have practised enough with single sentences, you can move on to writing sentences together in a paragraph.

As you write, remember to:

- Be careful about your handwriting. Don't worry about grammar or vocabulary.
- Start each sentence with an upper-case letter.
- Make your letters the same size.
- Make ascenders and descenders the same length.
- Keep equal spaces between words.
- Finish your sentences with a full stop.

Here is an example paragraph:

I work as a nurse in a hospital. My job is very difficult, but I love it. I like helping people and taking care of them. The hospital is often busy and noisy. I have to stay calm at these times.

Now write out this example paragraph on the lines below. Try to keep your letters and spaces the same size every time.

I work as a nurse

In this example paragraph, two people are writing about their daughter:

Our daughter is a wonderful person. She is studying to be a teacher. She cooks for us every Sunday. She laughs and smiles all the time. We love her very much.

Write out this example paragraph on the lines below.

Our daughter

This example paragraph is about a flat:

I live in a lovely little two-bedroom flat in Bristol. I love it because it has a small garden, where I can sit and enjoy a nice cup of coffee in the mornings. Perfect!

Write out this example paragraph on the lines below.

I live in

32

Complete the short paragraphs

On this page, let's complete the paragraphs by writing in the missing words. The missing words are all written above the paragraph. You have to choose which word goes in which blank space, and write it in carefully. Sometimes the blank spaces need a single word, sometimes a group of words.

Complete each paragraph by filling in the blank spaces with the words or groups of words listed above the paragraph.

live   tired   drink   wake up

Coffee is the best _____ in the world. It tastes and smells so good. When I am _____, it helps me to _____. I don't think I could _____ without coffee!

summer   club   air   friends

I love _____. In the summer, it's great to be outside in the fresh ____. I play tennis with my _____, or with the other people at my tennis ____.

Again, fill in the blank spaces in each paragraph with the words or groups of words listed above the paragraph.

train   clients   each way   long
8.30 am   emails   tired   meetings

John's work day is very _____. He takes the _____ to work. The journey lasts one hour _____. He arrives at his office at _____. He has lots of _____ every day, and he also needs to check all his _____ and call his _____. John often leaves the office at 8 pm, and by this time he is very _____.

New York   buildings   love
exciting   visit   pancakes

My favourite city in the world is _____. It is a really _____ place. I like eating _____ for breakfast, and seeing all the _____ lit up at night. Every time I _____ New York, I find new things that I _____ about it.

33

Write your own short paragraphs

Now you can work on writing your own paragraphs.

Here is an example paragraph about London:

London is a very interesting city. It has many famous buildings. You can see Big Ben, St. Paul's Cathedral and the London Eye. It is a very busy place. There are many restaurants and theatres. It is never boring in London.

Write your own paragraph about a city on the lines below. You can use ideas and words from the example paragraph above to help you get started.

_____

_____

_____

_____

_____

_____

Now read this example paragraph about a good friend called Anne:

Anne is one of my best friends. She has dark brown hair and brown eyes. She is tall and has a nice smile. Anne is from Ireland. She is a writer, and she loves to read. At the weekend, Anne and I often go shopping. I can call her at any time, and talk to her about any problem. She is a very friendly person.

On the lines below, write a paragraph about a friend or family member. The important thing is your handwriting, not your grammar and vocabulary.

_____

_____

_____

_____

_____

_____

_____

_____

34

Complete the long paragraphs

This section will practise writing longer paragraphs. You will fill in gaps in the paragraphs to complete them.

This paragraph below is about learning English. Look at the words listed above the paragraph. Choose which word (or group of words) goes in which blank space.

English   language   on the internet

speak   international   make friends

opportunities   jobs

English is a very important _____ for me to study. You need to speak English well for many ____ in my country. If you learn to _____ English well, you can often find interesting _____ in other countries too. Many people all over the world speak English. It is an _____ language. I like talking to people in other countries _____. There are lots of websites and chatrooms where many people speak English. I like to _____ with people who speak English. I can practise my _____ with them, and have a nice chat at the same time!

This paragraph is about exercise. Fill in the gaps with the words (or groups of words) listed above the paragraph.

better   bad day   healthy   fitness
strong   lungs   run   time
a few minutes   exercise   a bike ride
heart   healthy weight   stress

Exercise is very important for staying _____.
Many people spend too much _____ sitting in
front of a TV or a computer screen. Studies
show that just _____ of exercise each
day can really improve your _____.
Exercise has many positive effects. First, it
can help to keep your _____ and _____
healthy. Second, exercise can make your
muscles _____ and flexible. Third, it can help
people to stay at a _____. Last
of all, people who regularly _____ often
say that it helps to reduce their _____ levels.
If you are having a _____, going for a
___, a swim or _____ can make you feel
so much _____.

35

Write your own long paragraphs

Now let's practise writing longer paragraphs about different subjects.

In the first paragraph, write about a place where you have lived. To help you get started, you can use some of the vocabulary words below. Of course, you can use your own words if you prefer.

park	buildings	church	town
mosque	traffic	beautiful	busy
noisy	school	city	quiet
village	shops	hospital	museum

Write on the lines below. Do not worry about grammar or spelling. The important thing is that your handwriting is clear and easy to read when you write longer paragraphs.

_____

_____

_____

_____

_____

_____

_____

_____

_____

_____

In the second paragraph, write about your home. There are some words below, to give you ideas about what you can write. You can use as many of these words as you like, and of course you can add your own.

living room   bathroom   toilet   hall

window   garden   balcony   kitchen

carpet   curtains   bedroom   sofa

table   fireplace

Write on the lines below. Remember to write carefully and use correct spacing.

_____

_____

_____

_____

_____

_____

_____

_____

_____

_____

'Real world' joined-up writing exercises 1

Over the next four pages, you will practise joined-up writing in 'real world' situations.

Joined-up writing is what we use to write most of the time. It is best to use joined-up writing when you have to write quickly.

Thank-you note

First, you are going to write a thank-you note. There is an example of a good thank-you note on page 36 of this book. You can look back at this example to help you.

Think of something nice that someone has done for you, and write to them to say thank you for it. It could be a present, a good English lesson or something else kind or helpful.

Dear _____ (name)

_____

_____

_____

_____

_____

_____

Yours,

_____ (your name)

Taking notes

It is important that you can write quickly and carefully, so that in everyday life people can easily read your writing. If you are studying, it is also important to be able to take notes quickly, to follow what your teacher says in class. Joined-up writing is perfect for this situation.

Let's practise this skill. Find a short radio or TV programme, or an online video, and take notes about it as you watch.

There is an example of notes written in good joined-up handwriting on page 36 of this book. You can look back at this example to help you.

Use the space below to take notes in joined-up writing. Try to write quickly, but still carefully enough that someone else could easily read what you have written.

'Real world' joined-up writing exercises 2

Writing in a diary

Another great way to practise your joined-up writing is by writing in a diary. A diary is a book where you can write about your day, your life and your feelings. It is very good writing practice and helps you to see how your handwriting in English is getting better over time. Try to start a diary and write in it every day if you can!

First, write a diary page about your day. Write about what you did, what you ate, where you went, who you talked to, or anything else! Don't worry about grammar, spelling and vocabulary – the important thing is to write quickly and carefully.

Monday
28

Here is another diary page. Use this diary page to write about something that happened in your life. Here are some ideas for what to write about:

- The best day of your life

- Your earliest memory

- A holiday or celebration

- An important achievement or event

Again, remember to write carefully but also quite quickly.

Wednesday

14

Word scramble

This book can't be all work and no play, so let's play some games! These games will help you practise your handwriting while you have some fun.

Word scramble

Look at the words below – the letters are in the wrong order! Write them into the correct order in the blank spaces underneath.

You should use print letters to fill in the unscrambled words. When letters stand alone, and cannot join up to any other letters, they should be written as print letters.

Here is an example of what to do:

gdo

d o g

nsu

_ _ _

riwte

_ _ _ _ _

sdetunt

_ _ _ _ _ _ _

fiocfe

_ _ _ _ _ _

lebat

_ _ _ _ _

natri

_ _ _ _ _

ehuso

_ _ _ _ _

nawmo

_ _ _ _ _

liepnc

_ _ _ _ _ _

yitc

_ _ _ _

Number sudoku

Sudoku is a fun puzzle game to practise writing your numbers. Playing sudoku is very simple.

- Each row of 9 numbers must have all numbers from 1 to 9. They don't have to be in order.
- Each column of 9 numbers must have all numbers from 1 to 9. They don't have to be in order.
- Each 3 x 3 small section of the 9 x 9 square must have all numbers from 1 to 9.

Some of the numbers have already been filled in. Trace (write over) each number to see clearly what it is. Then you can work out where to put the rest of the numbers to complete the puzzle.

6		2	3			8		
	8		2			6		7
	7		6		4		1	
		1		7	6	9		
4	5						7	8
		7	1	4		3		
	4		5		9		6	
1		5			8		9	
		3			2	7		5

	5		9		1		7	
6								1
		7	3		8	6		
	7		4	1	3		5	
	3						4	
	8		5	2	7		1	
		9	8		5	4		
4								3
	6		7		2		9	

Crossword

The crossword puzzle is a popular way to spend a Sunday afternoon. Read the clues and write the answers in the numbered spaces on the crossword. There is a number in brackets after each one of the clues. This is the number of letters in the answer word.

You should use upper-case letters to fill in the crossword. People complete crosswords with upper-case letters so that their answers are clear and easy to read.

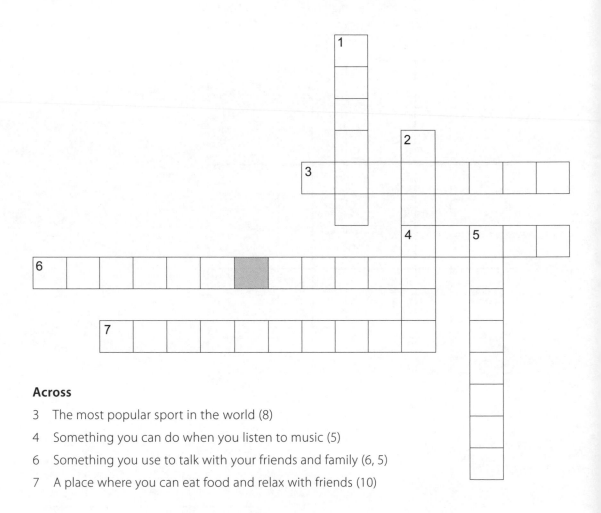

Across

3   The most popular sport in the world (8)

4   Something you can do when you listen to music (5)

6   Something you use to talk with your friends and family (6, 5)

7   A place where you can eat food and relax with friends (10)

Down

1   The capital of England (6)

2   A person who goes to a school and studies (7)

5   Something you write in when you are in class (8)

Wordsearch

This wordsearch is great practice for your handwriting. You must find the words below. The words are in straight lines forwards, backwards, up and down. However, before you can circle the words, you have to trace (write over) each print letter.

study   vocabulary   review

practise   pencil

language   handwriting   notebook

erase   sentence

g	o	t	e	u	n	l	d	s	t	u	d	y
m	t	l	a	n	g	u	a	g	e	v	q	p
r	q	v	k	t	o	m	l	m	g	e	m	x
k	o	o	b	e	t	o	n	a	n	c	l	q
n	h	c	s	a	c	d	j	o	t	n	e	s
f	y	a	r	c	f	m	d	t	t	e	s	l
e	r	b	r	z	b	d	o	c	i	t	i	e
z	a	u	e	m	f	d	i	t	r	n	t	r
s	h	l	v	u	v	w	r	o	w	e	c	a
a	z	a	i	m	s	j	k	w	d	s	a	s
p	r	r	e	t	m	p	w	h	n	u	r	e
n	y	y	w	a	v	o	k	l	a	b	p	b
a	l	t	c	n	e	p	m	h	h	w	h	j

Puzzle solutions

Page 76

sun	write
student	office
table	train
house	woman
pencil	city

Page 77

6	1	2	3	5	7	8	4	9
5	8	4	2	9	1	6	3	7
3	7	9	6	8	4	5	1	2
2	3	1	8	7	6	9	5	4
4	5	6	9	2	3	1	7	8
8	9	7	1	4	5	3	2	6
7	4	8	5	3	9	2	6	1
1	2	5	7	6	8	4	9	3
9	6	3	4	1	2	7	8	5

3	5	2	9	6	1	8	7	4
6	9	8	2	7	4	5	3	1
1	4	7	3	5	8	6	2	9
2	7	6	4	1	3	9	5	8
5	3	1	6	8	9	2	4	7
9	8	4	5	2	7	3	1	6
7	1	9	8	3	5	4	6	2
4	2	5	1	9	6	7	8	3
8	6	3	7	4	2	1	9	5

Page 78

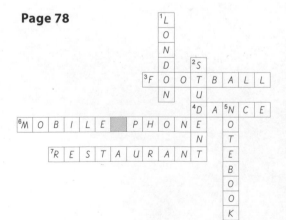

Page 79

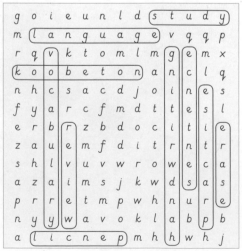